the | **Institute**
for | **Employment**
| **Studies**

From People to Profits

L Barber
S Hayday
S Bevan

Supported by the IES
Research
Club

Report 355

Published by:

THE INSTITUTE FOR EMPLOYMENT STUDIES
Mantell Building
Falmer
Brighton BN1 9RF
UK

Tel.   + 44 (0) 1273 686751
Fax   + 44 (0) 1273 690430

http://www.employment-studies.co.uk

British Cataloguing-in-Publication Data

A catalogue record for this publication is available from the British Library

ISBN 1-85184-284-5

Printed in Great Britain by IKON Office Solutions plc

FROM PEOPLE TO PROFITS

Other titles from IES:

Attendance Management: a review of good practice
Bevan S, Hayday S
IES Report 353, 1998. ISBN 1-85184-282-9

Breaking the Long Hours Culture
Kodz J, Kersley B, Strebler M T, O'Regan S
IES Report 352, 1998. ISBN 1-85184-281-0

Keeping the Best: A Practical Guide to Retaining Key Employees
Bevan S, Barber L, Robinson D
IES Report 337, 1997. ISBN 1-85184-265-9

Getting the Best out of your Competencies
Strebler M T, Robinson D, Heron P
IES Report 334, 1997. ISBN 1-85184-260-8

From Admin to Strategy: the Changing Face of the HR Function
Tamkin P, Barber L, Dench S
IES Report 332, 1997. ISBN 1-85184-263-2

Who Cares? The business benefits of carer-friendly practices
Bevan S, Kettley P, Patch A
IES Report 330, 1997. ISBN 1-85184-258-6

Outsourcing: a Flexible Option for the Future?
Reilly P, Tamkin P
IES Report 320, 1997. ISBN 1-85184-247-0

A catalogue of these and over 100 other titles is available from IES, or on the IES Website, www.employment-studies.co.uk

The Institute for Employment Studies

IES is an independent, international and apolitical centre of research and consultancy in human resource issues. It works closely with employers in the manufacturing, service and public sectors, government departments, agencies, professional and employee bodies, and foundations. For 30 years the Institute has been a focus of knowledge and practical experience in employment and training policy, the operation of labour markets and human resource planning and development. IES is a not-for-profit organisation which has a multidisciplinary staff of over 50. IES expertise is available to all organisations through research, consultancy and publications.

IES aims to help bring about sustainable improvements in employment policy and human resource management. IES achieves this by increasing the understanding and improving the practice of key decision makers in policy bodies and employing organisations.

The IES Research Club

This report is the product of a study supported by the IES Research Club, through which a group of IES Corporate Members finance, and often participate in, applied research on employment issues. The members of the Club are:

Anglian Water
BAA plc
Barclays Bank plc
The Benefits Agency
BOC Group
BBC
British Steel plc
BT plc
Cabinet Office
Department for the Environment,
   Transport and Regions
Electricity Association
Glaxo Wellcome plc
Guardian Insurance
Halifax plc
HM Customs & Excise

Home Office
Inland Revenue
Littlewoods Organisation plc
Lloyds TSB Group
Marks & Spencer plc
NatWest UK
NHS Executive
Orange plc
Post Office
Rolls-Royce plc
J Sainsbury plc
Shell UK Ltd
Standard Life
Unilever UK (Holdings) Ltd
Woolwich plc

Acknowledgements

We would like to thank the case study organisation for releasing their company data to us. Without their co-operation and openness this study would not have been possible. The authors are also indebted to Dr Dale Griffin of the University of Sussex for his invaluable support and advice throughout this project.

Contents

Executive Summary

Most service sector businesses want to maximise customer satisfaction. This is because they believe that happy customers spend more and stay loyal. Many businesses also believe that happy employees contribute to customer satisfaction, arguing that effective staff management can, indirectly, affect sales and profits. This link between employees, customers and profits has been called the service-profit chain.

This report presents an empirical test of the service-profit chain in a large UK retail business. Based on data gathered from 65,000 employees and 25,000 customers from almost 100 individual stores, the study, conducted by the Institute for Employment Studies, has shown that:

- The service-profit chain has a sound empirical basis; there is a link between employee satisfaction, customer satisfaction and an increase in sales.

- Customer satisfaction in itself, however, represents a weak link in the chain unless it is accompanied by customer loyalty (*ie* an intention to spend again).

- Employee satisfaction and, more specifically, employee commitment to the company, directly affect sales increases. It also affects sales through improved customer loyalty and improved staff attendance.

- This study shows that a one point increase in employee commitment can lead to a monthly increase of up to £200,000 in sales per store.

The report deals with important issues for service sector businesses:

1. Customer satisfaction, without customer loyalty, is not enough to improve business performance.

2. Despite their stated desire to maximise customer satisfaction, many businesses are using inadequate or poor measures of its strength.

3. Human resource management in the service sector has a significant part to play. The study has demonstrated the importance of a positive organisation culture, good line management, employee commitment and employee attendance to the effective working of the service-profit chain.

4. Data of the kind used in the study can be readily used to develop performance indicators for the service-profit chain. However, most service sector businesses do not collect or analyse the necessary data.

1. Introduction

1.1 Background

Service sector businesses constantly strive to improve upon the service they offer to customers in order to remain competitive. The links between customer retention and profitability have been clear for some time, and achieving high levels of customer satisfaction and retention are prime objectives for most organisations. Relationship marketing and monitoring customer satisfaction have been key activities for marketing functions and are critical to understanding and securing customer retention.

Organisations invest considerable sums of money in promoting and achieving a good customer service. As a result, a variety of loyalty schemes have emerged, and call centre operations and customer service departments have mushroomed. At the same time organisations have embarked upon various customer care and quality initiatives in order to gain repeat business, to retain and grow their market share. In addition, it might be reasonable to expect that the quality and nature of the service relationship that exists between customer and employee may also prove critical to business performance.

Among the emerging factors now felt to be linked to positive customer reactions and behaviour are employee satisfaction and commitment, (particularly in sectors where price and product quality can be emulated by competitors). Customer and employee attitude surveys are common tools within many organisations. However, employers are beginning to recognise (or become curious about) the potential added value of linking customer and employee attitude survey data to complement traditional financial measures, in order to gain a holistic view of their businesses.

Although employee attitudes, customer satisfaction and organisational performance have all received considerable individual attention, only recently have the interrelations between all three become of particular interest to organisations. In our work for large companies, IES has more frequently been called upon to provide insights on the links between business performance and employee contributions. Through the IES Research Club of 30 large employers, IES received support for a research study to investigate the empirical basis for this so-called 'attitude chain'. At the start of this work we were particularly keen to pinpoint literature which directly addressed the subject of relating employee and customer attitudes to profitability, and we were struck by the lack of research reporting the inter-relations between them. Our review also led us to believe that further research in this area was feasible and apt, as relatively little work has been done anywhere, and almost none in the UK (chapter two offers a summary of the key readings we identified).

An important and timely article for our research was that of Rucci, Kirn and Quinn (1998) which outlines the American company Sears' creation of an attitude model and its use in rescuing its failing business. The Sears model relates and quantifies the effects of changes in employee attitudes on customers' impressions of Sears, through to the business outcome indicators of return on assets, operating margins and revenue growth. Using this model they are able to predict the effects of a change in employee and customer attitudes on sales income. They have such confidence in the model that it is used to assess the performance of their staff and the payment of bonuses!

Other authors such as Paradise-Tornow (1991) and Schneider (1991) maintain that people-centred management approaches require long-term commitment from businesses and may therefore not result in financial performance in the short term. In addition, Wiley (1991) and Silvestro (1999) found staff to be more satisfied in less profitable stores! Recent publications, Patterson *et al.* (1997), and Caffman and Harter (1998) also showed the positive influence and impact that employees might have upon aspects of business performance, via people management practices. The work of Caffman and Harter (1998) considered employee engagement to be a leading indicator and found it linked with tangible business outcomes.

Informed by both the literature and working with organisations, we were curious to learn more about the effects that people management might have upon customers and financial performance. Given that:

- selection and recruitment
- induction and training
- staff development
- performance management
- communication

has largely been devolved to the line, we were particularly curious to learn more about which aspects of employee and customer satisfaction might mediate, and result in, improved business performance.

Previous work[1] has led IES to believe that frequency of employee absence and employee commitment are linked. We were interested in understanding further the consequences that employee behaviour such as unwanted absence and turnover may have in relation to customer behaviour (such as loyalty), business performance, and what the implications might be for human resource management.

As part of our study, employee, customer and performance data collected by a major retailer over a period of two years were released to IES. Detailed statistical analyses were conducted to test the validity of the theoretical model we had devised from the literature and our knowledge gained from working with service sector organisations.

The main focus of this IES study was to explore the relevant employee attitudes that might underpin employee and customer behaviours associated with improved business performance. We were particularly keen to explore such links given that interventions intended to improve the service relationship between employee and customer may be focused on either or both.

---

[1]   Bevan S, Hayday S (1998), *Attendance Management: A review of good practice*, IES Report 353

1.2 Objectives

IES knows from working with organisations that service sector employers are keen to understand more about the links between employee attitudes, customer satisfaction and organisational performance. Given such interest, together with a paucity of reported empirical research, IES was sponsored by the IES Research Club to explore such links. The key research question this study sought to address therefore concerned whether it is possible to relate employee attitudes, through customer satisfaction, to business performance. Our objectives were defined thus:

- To determine appropriate measures of business performance.
- To examine the nature and quality of existing employee, customer and business performance data held by one or two case study organisations.
- To explore the relationships between employee attitudes, customer satisfaction and business performance.
- To make suggestions regarding the management of data collection practices.

1.3 Literature review

A review of the literature was undertaken to identify and learn from previous studies concerning employee attitudes, customer satisfaction and business performance. The issue of how the job attitudes of employees are related to the satisfaction of customers, and through this to the financial performance of the organisation, is one that has attracted surprisingly little interest until the past couple of years. There are considerable bodies of literature on the components of both customer and employee satisfaction, but only a few research studies attempt to investigate the inter-relations between them, and even fewer link these two items to business outcomes.

A search of psychological, marketing research and business databases has produced a surprisingly small amount of literature addressing these subjects. The majority of studies are American with the work of Benjamin Schneider and James Heskett dominating. Throughout all the studies there is debate around the issue of how the indicators of satisfaction and performance should be constructed. These methodological questions will not be covered in this review as they these require considerable separate discussion. However a good overview of the topic is given in Schneider, Ashworth, Higgs and Carr (1996). The studies almost exclusively are based on data from service organisations such as banks and retail stores, and consider only external customers.

1.4 Employee attitudes and customer satisfaction

The positive interaction between the employee's view of the way the organisation functions and the customer's perception of service quality is described in papers by Schneider, Parkington and Buxton (1980), Schneider (1990), Burke, Borucki and Hurley (1992) and Johnson (1996). These emphasise that employees will give good service when such behaviour is expected and rewarded by the organisation, and crucially that it has practices that enable its delivery (*ie* training, product knowledge/briefing *etc.*). Tompkins (1992) stresses the importance of line management and comments that 'it is critical that managers have the training and tools to understand the role they are to play and the expectations of employees who work for them'. The need for the creation of a service climate to begin at the top of an organisation is discussed in Schmit and Allscheid (1995), with management support for service imperatives and concern for employees' welfare being essential.

The importance of the HR function in managing employees' experiences within the organisation so that these are positively reflected in their dealings with customers is covered by Ulrich, Halbrook, Meder, Stuchlik and Thorp (1991). This paper also stresses the requirement that the HR function has a role in strategic management. The importance of HR expertise in implementing changes in employee attitudes towards customer service is illustrated in Stewart (1999). She explains in a brief, practical paper how Little Chef have utilised customer surveys to link customer satisfaction with performance management tools. HR managers are able to identify which aspects of an individual's performance need development and are able to then provide suitable support.

Schneider and Bowen (1993) raise the interesting issue that the definition of good service varies according to the market sector, for example the need for speed and efficiency at McDonald's would be totally inappropriate in an expensive restaurant. They conclude it is essential to recruit suitable staff for specific roles. There are no universal criteria of good service that can be applied to all organisations. The improvement in the ability to perform a job well and attain both job and customer satisfaction will vary with the employee's length of tenure, as is shown in the work of Schlesinger and Zornitsky (1991). Both Weaver (1994) and Fredendall and Robbins (1995) highlight the importance of the empowerment of employees to use their initiative to meet customer demands, although the appropriateness of this depends on the environment.

1.5 Employee attitudes and organisational performance

Only seven articles among those collected investigate the effect of employee attitudes on organisational performance and most of these have been published in the last couple of years. Research by Patterson *et al.* (1997) among 67 small to medium sized manufacturers, showed that people management practices accounted for 19 per cent of the variation in change in profitability between companies. Job satisfaction and employee commitment was also demonstrated to influence profitability. They conclude that 'people and their attitudes to their jobs are the most important company assets'. Benkhoff (1997) found that employee commitment to the organisation is significantly related to the financial success of branches in a study of a German bank network. Supervisory commitment was shown to have a particularly strong impact on the outcome indicators.

A review of the Gallup Organisation's database by Caffman and Harter (1998) looked across a wide variety of businesses and identified human resource issues that were important to every organisation. They found that successful companies or units have different profiles of employee perceptions from those that are less successful. In these there were employees who had clear expectations, close relationships, feel that what they do relates to 'something significant' and that they can contribute to this while learning and developing as individuals. They focused upon employee engagement as a leading business indicator and their research concludes with the recommendation that organisations should identify and study areas of success within themselves.

A paper by Ostroff (1992) correlates employee satisfaction and attitudes with performance at the organisational level. She found that organisations with more satisfied employees were more effective than those with less happy staff. An article by Paradise-Tornow (1991) examined leadership and management in retail banking by relating bank managers' performances to those of their branches. This found that staff perception of leadership was most positively related to profit. Curiously, management effectiveness was strongly negatively correlated to performance. This finding she explains by a trade-off between achieving short-term financial results by leadership, against people-centred management actions, which show longer term, advantages. Reflecting this finding, recent unpublished work by Silvestro (1999) identified a negative relationship between employee satisfaction and store profitability. Staff in the six stores studied were found to be happier in the less profitable stores, which were smaller and less stressful in contrast to the larger, busy stores where they were subjected to greater supervision and pressure.

1.6 Employee and customer attitudes and organisational performance

The literature search has revealed little published work that attempts to relate organisational performance to employee and customer satisfaction. In 1997 Heskett, Sasser and Schlesinger produced 'the service profit chain' which first clearly described the model of employee attitudes influencing customer satisfaction and through this, impacting on sales and profits. They describe the notion of a 'satisfaction mirror' in which employee satisfaction results in customer satisfaction, which then leads to enhanced employee job satisfaction. This benefits the organisation through increased sales. The authors rely on supplying evidence for the separate links in the chain from various sources rather than formally evaluating the whole model in just one organisation. The recent article by Rucci, Kirn and Quinn (1998), in contrast, outlines the successful creation by the American retail company Sears, of an attitude chain model from employee to customer through to sales revenue. As mentioned earlier in the introduction to this report, the IES research project has used a similar approach. Three other useful articles were published in a special volume of *Human Resource Planning* devoted to service quality and organisational effectiveness which was edited by Schneider.

Tornow and Wiley (1991) found that the maximum impact on organisational performance was made when leadership values and local management practices were consistent, so that a single service-quality approach is visible to both employees and customers. Data over two years were collected by Ryan, Schmit and Johnson (1996) from an automobile finance company. These revealed that teamwork, training, and job/company satisfaction were related to performance. A link between customer and employee attitudes and productivity existed, but although this was small it could have a large effect on profits. An interesting study by Wiley (1991) took a hard look at a supportive work environment and its impact on financial performance. He discovered that the favourable views of employees were weakly negatively related to financial results, and stores which had strong financial results achieved weaker satisfaction ratings. The rather depressing, although logical conclusion from this was that providing what customers and staff see as the highest levels of satisfaction and service might come at a cost to the organisation.

Schneider (1991) gives a useful review of the subject area in a summary article in the *Human Resource Planning* issue devoted to this topic. His view is that employee and customer attitudes can be related to profits, but that this is not always the case. The implications of the research are that the age and the developmental stage of an organisation will affect the service it provides and its profitability. The beneficial effects of more experienced staff, low absenteeism, low turnover and product developments will take some time to become apparent in organisational performance. A long-term view needs to be taken. A commitment to service is essential throughout the organisation from the top down. Clarity about the organisation's market position and the type of service this requires is needed, together with the HR practices that match this.

Schneider concludes that 'it is a long way from employee attitudes to organisational financial performance' and that much of the work that has been conducted has been too simplistic. However, if various factors are taken sensibly into account it is possible to relate attitudes to profitability. This suggested that further research in the area was feasible and worthwhile, as relatively little work has been done and even less in the UK. The key areas appear to be highlighting the specific employee attitudes that promote good customer service and the measures to encourage them that can be taken by the organisation.

The Institute for Employment Studies

2. The IES Attitude Chain Theoretical Model

It should be remembered that our key research objective was to learn whether it might be possible to relate employee attitudes through customer satisfaction, to business performance, and that we were dependant on making use of existing data. Causal or pathway modelling, as the Sears example clearly demonstrates, requires careful consideration regarding the nature of data to be captured in order for it to become an operational tool. It should also be remembered that it took Sears five years to achieve! Given the exploratory nature of our research, which had to be completed in just six months, we designed our model to fit a 'typical' service sector organisation and at this stage was still a prototype rather than bespoke. The Sears experience illustrates that 'one size does not fit all' and models need to be tailored, modified and revised in order to fit and meet different organisations' needs and culture.

Influenced by the Sears example, IES developed a theoretical model capable of supporting relevant measures of employee attitude, customer satisfaction and business performance data of interest to us. The process of building the model forced us to be absolutely clear (*a priori*) about the data requirements sought from any case study organisation. In order to conduct the appropriate statistical analysis these data needed to meet the following criteria:

- be available for at least 100 units, branches or establishments
- hold employee and customer survey data sets — captured over the same time periods
- have a range of business performance measures — for the same or ideally longer time periods
- be portable — in order to be made accessible to IES.

2.1 Approach

The key stages of the research are reflected in the remaining chapters of this report:

- Chapter Three (the Scoping Stage) describes our experiences of securing our case study organisation.

- Chapter Four (a Case Study) summarises the analysis of the data sets released to IES by the case study organisation and describes the final model generated.

- Chapter Five (Discussion) offers pragmatic advice and considers the research findings in relation to HR policy and practice.

Figure 2.1 shows that we sought data typically captured via employee and customer attitude surveys, and metrics commonly used to determine and monitor aspects of business performance. Multivariate data analysis procedures are usually exploratory and descriptive by nature, whereas causal or pathway modelling requires a confirmatory approach based upon path modelling.

The theoretical model served to guide model testing in the data analysis phase. Path modelling (more formally, *structural equation modelling*) is a technique that estimates and tests a fully specified theoretical causal model. Thus, the model-estimation phase is entirely controlled by the model-definition phase. Path modelling takes a given causal ordering of variables and tests which of the relations between the variables (which can be either direct or indirect) are 'significantly' large. A direct relationship is one in which, for example, employee commitment is assumed to directly affect employee behaviour; an indirect relationship is one in which employee commitment acting through employee behaviour affects customer satisfaction. In general, the model-estimation phase is not designed to test whether the *causal* implications of the model are correct—the hypothesised causal ordering is *assumed* to be correct, and the relations within that model are then estimated. Note that the input to the model is a set of observed correlations, and in general, the correlations between variables cannot lead to inferences of causality. Figure 2.1 therefore served to commit the investigators to a given causal ordering: one deemed highly defensible by those involved. Note that within a given causal ordering, it is still possible to examine whether the assumed relationships are direct or indirect.

The Institute for Employment Studies

Figure 2.1 The IES hypothetical attitude chain model

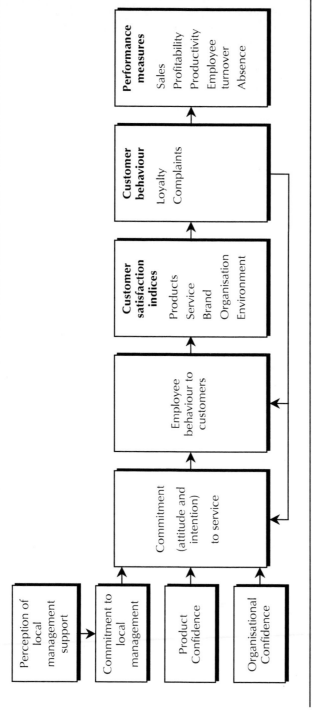

Source: IES

Once the model was specified, the next step was to find appropriate data to allow the model to be estimated. Although the IES model sought a variety of measures, we were well aware that finding a case study organisation that currently captured the full range of metrics specified was unlikely.

3. The Scoping Stage

We were fortunate that such was the strength of interest shown by members of the IES Research Club that we were approached by ten organisations expressing interest with regard to participating in this study. As we believed, the notion of being able to relate attitudes to profitability was of real interest to them and a number already were already collecting information regarding employee attitudes, customer satisfaction and business performance.

We acknowledge that in some sectors, such as manufacturing, the notion of 'the customer' can be difficult to define or determine, and therefore further analysis of company data using our theoretical model within some organisations may not be possible. In addition, a few employers we spoke with were curious about the notion of extending our model to include the HR function and their internal customers, but the model as we have defined it is dependent on and only concerned with the views of external customers. Other statistical analyses or models may be appropriate where the customer is not external or other requirements of this particular model cannot be met.

The scoping stage of the study aimed to identify and secure suitable case study organisations within a service sector organisation, such as financial services or retail. IES research methodology often involves a number of case studies, but we sought to enlist no more than two case studies, as we required access to information that had been captured at an establishment level (*eg* branches or stores) within an organisation.

In order to identify potential case study organisations we sought to understand from volunteering organisations:

- the details, findings and outcomes of any employee and customer surveys conducted
- the nature and utility of key performance business indicators employed
- what links or assumptions organisations currently made regarding employee attitudes, customer satisfaction and business performance, and the nature of any relationships found
- who owned, managed or had responsibility for the above data sources.

Most of the ten volunteer organisations had some experience of conducting surveys and they also had a number of performance measures in place. Several companies had well established processes for collecting and analysing the information they collect, and the notion of further analysis of these data proved very appealing to them. However, we discovered a number of barriers that prevented further analysis of their existing data.

We found that a number of companies held data that had only captured the views of:

- managers
- key account holders
- occasional 'mystery shoppers'

or had only developed measures for specific units such as:

- head offices
- certain locations
- pilot sites.

In addition some companies:

- measured customer or employee satisfaction on an *ad hoc* basis
- did not hold sufficient data at an establishment level
- had 'gaps' in their existing data sets or had changed their processes and practices for data collection
- had not collected information over the same time periods
- collected attitude data but no customer survey data (or vice versa)
- did not currently hold aggregated unit level data
- employed processes or measures that varied at a local level.

The scoping stage of our research project proved critical in order to secure a case study organisation that could provide us with data that met the requirements of our attitude chain model. The barriers we encountered were found to cluster around three main themes regarding aspects of data management:

- compatibility
- reliability
- consistency.

Just one company, a major retailer, held data that appeared to meet the requirements of our Attitude Chain model. We learned that:

- customer satisfaction had been collected consistently for just under one year
- employee attitude data had also been collected using the same questionnaire for two years
- a number of business performance measures were in place.

4. A Case Study

Our case study company was already aware of the potential value of being able to link attitudes and business performance and was keen to establish whether some 'empirical weight' could be found to add to what seemed intuitive or common sense. The company had already undertaken some further analysis of their data, which although limited, produced findings that were encouraging and worthy of further investigation. The analysis we proposed to conduct demanded complex data analysis techniques and we planned to explore their data at a much greater level of detail via our model.

Early discussions with a representative from the company revealed that the data we sought for further analysis was not held by one person or managed centrally. Although these data were 'owned' by the organisation, various departments and different individuals were responsible for managing the collection and utilisation of these data. We therefore made contact with a number of personnel, including the external contractor who conducts the employee attitude survey for the company in order to ensure that any data sets released were compatible and consistent with our model.

Our main objective at this stage of the research was to create a single data set containing employee attitudes, customer satisfaction and business performance measures for the same stores for the same time periods which could be fed into our model. As 'establishment' was our unit of analysis we needed to:

- identify which stores had collected customer satisfaction data
- match these stores with relevant employee satisfaction data during the same time period

- gain access to business performance measures employed during the same time period for these stores.

4.1 Data manipulation

Of necessity, this had to be a retrospective study working with existing data to explore what was possible. Testing the model to confirm which datasets were causal influences and which were outcome variables would have ideally required systematic data collection over time. It would have also been preferable to design the attitude surveys to include items that we wished to test in the model. However, to conduct the research in an ideal way would have taken considerably longer than the six months available for this project! We faced a number of technical challenges, which proved time consuming and involved numerous conversations with those responsible for releasing data to us. Our model required about one hundred data sets relating to retail outlets for analysis; we finally achieved ninety-one, which was adequate for descriptive purposes.

The stores with sets of both employee and customer attitude data were identified and made available to us. This provided a large database of 65,000 employees and 25,000 customers. It was then necessary to investigate what other information could be gathered to assess the performance of the selected stores. The case study organisation currently collects and monitors a number of performance measures and, most importantly, had done so consistently for those stores selected for at least two years. Four data sets were judged as being suitable outcome indicators for exploring the relationship between customers and employees:

- cash sales figures
- absence data
- staff turnover
- customer complaints.

Employee, customer, absence, complaints and sales data were available to us electronically. Staff turnover data, however, needed to be prepared from paper records by IES. We believed the effort spent producing the turnover data to be a good investment, as retaining key staff is an issue that is very much on the agenda of most employers and could potentially add considerable value to our research study.

The regional structure of the stores was also supplied to IES and it also seemed worthwhile to include this information in the data analysis, as this was thought to be a likely source of variation. Additionally, the employee survey included questions about individuals' working patterns and demographic details, which provided insight into the effects of different mixes of staff.

Data collection practices proved be an issue during the scoping stage of our research and we also found collecting the data from our case study organisation proved a much longer process than could have been anticipated. Collecting and converting the data released into a form suitable for analysis actually took longer than the development of the final model! The major problem, which is one that will apply to most organisations, is that one department or place does not hold the information. Each set of information is collected for a specific purpose and generally remains with that area of the business. It might be imagined that a large combined computer dataset would be held centrally, but this was not the situation in our case study organisation, or in the organisations that we approached in our scoping study.

Once the appropriate department and contact person within the organisation had been identified and the data supplied, the next task was to extract the information required for the model. This involved further discussions with the organisation about how the data was collected, its reliability, and which items would prove most suitable for the research. As we had to be absolutely clear about the reliability of any data we used we decided to include:

● only permanent staff turnover — which IES had prepared from paper records

● only those store complaints that could be influenced directly by the store — so checkout errors were included but product complaints were not

● the total of paid and unpaid hours — reflecting all non-attendance across the stores was judged to be the most suitable measure of absence available.

We excluded:

● students and temporary employees from staff turnover — as there was a clear seasonal pattern to their employment

● any stores that had opened or closed during the given time period — as the views of their employees and customers were likely to be atypical.

Before the analysis could begin we also needed to convert the separate data files into a form that could be used by the model. This process also involved standardising much of the data into percentages and looking at changes over time.

4.2 Data analysis

The initial phase of the analysis centred on the employee survey results which included over fifty attitude questions and demographic information. Using statistical techniques, we clustered the responses to these questions into groups which more accurately described underlying factors. These groups or scales, complete details of which are given in Appendix 3, are better predictors of influences than just one item. The scales we identified were composed from the following items:

- employee satisfaction with line management — support given to staff, recognition of good work, giving feedback, listening, resolving problems and giving opportunities to grow and develop

- employee commitment — wanting to stay with the company, able to tell people that it's a good place to work, desire to do best work possible

- company culture — fair treatment, ability counting, caring for and respecting employees, well run company, friendly atmosphere.

It should be remembered that these scales were created from questions that had not been formulated for the purpose of this research, yet it was surprising how statistically reliable they were found to be. A scale concerning training was tested, but it was found to be weak, probably because its components were not ideal. A strong scale concerning employee commitment towards customer service would have been of value in our model but, again, it was not possible to create one from the existing survey questions.

Further analysis was then conducted in consultation with a statistician from The University of Sussex and involved specifying a causal path model based on the theoretical attitude chain model and then testing which of the hypothesised links between variables were statistically significant. The background to the analyses undertaken can be found in Appendix 2. Note that the feedback loop from customer behaviour to staff commitment could not be included in this model, because estimating such 'loops' requires more specialised data that were not available in the present case study.

Different measures of similar constructs were examined to see which led to the strongest findings. For example, the measures of customer satisfaction with service and likely future spending levels were better explanatory variables than customer overall satisfaction, and so only the first two were used in the final model. Indeed, as Reichheld (1996) highlights, 60-80 per cent of customers who defect to competitors claim in customer surveys to be 'satisfied' or 'very satisfied' before they take their custom elsewhere. Knowing that a customer is just generally 'satisfied' is no guarantee that they will remain loyal.

A very important consideration was the performance measure to be used for each store. Data on profits, which would probably be the ideal metric, were not available but cash sales by store had been supplied. However these, if unadjusted, are seriously distorted by such influences as store size, facilities and location. What was required was an indicator of a store's performance relative to its own track record. This was created using the trend of sales a year earlier to predict current sales. This notional current sales figure was then deducted from the actual figure, giving a measure of the extent to which the store was performing above or below expectation ('adjusted monthly sales').

Starting from a full model that included all possible direct and indirect links between selected variables, progressively simpler models were tested that systematically removed all weak and non-significant relations between variables. Thus, any item or influence, which was uncertain or weak, was removed.

4.3 Influences on the model

Upon initial examination of the correlations between variables, it was discovered that both staff turnover and customer complaints data were unrelated to the other major outcomes variables in this dataset (staff satisfaction, customer satisfaction, and sales performance) and so these two variables were eliminated from the path model.

In this sample, the major influence on staff turnover is the local labour market and conditions. The lack of relationship with the other variables suggests that there are either other influences affecting turnover, which have not been identified in the data available, or that there may be problems with the reliability of the information. To adequately explore staff turnover and its link to employee satisfaction would require thorough investigation of the data and possibly creating a specific model.

The failure of customer complaints as a reliable indicator of customer satisfaction was a surprise. Possible explanations include that the number of complaints relative to the number of customer transactions is small, or that the process for recording across the stores is not standardised. Further analysis of the reliability of these data would be required.

Two strong influences were identified which affected many of the other factors in the model, and if they had not been controlled would have confounded the interpretation of findings. Regional effects, as might be anticipated, were important. The differences in mean employee and customer satisfaction levels can be seen in table 4.1. The scale for both of these ranged from 0 'Extremely dissatisfied' to 10 'Extremely satisfied'. At the extremes there are the northern and southern regions: the fact of being in the north alone results in staff and customers being more satisfied than those in the south. Thus, the effects of region were statistically controlled in all analyses reported here.

Staff demographics also had some generalised effects across the model, so these were controlled for as well. Appendix 4 gives the details of the correlation coefficients for employee age, part-

Table 4.1 Regional effects on employee and customer satisfaction

Region	Mean overall employee satisfaction	Mean overall customer satisfaction
South	6.8	7.7
Central	7.0	7.8
East	7.3	7.9
Midlands	7.3	8.1
North	7.3	8.2
Total	**7.1**	**7.9**
	N=94	*N=94*

Source: IES, 1999

Table 4.2 Correlation between employee and customer attitudes and sales

	Customer satisfaction	Customer service satisfaction	Spending intention
Employee satisfaction	0.32	0.50	0.13
Employee commitment	0.42	0.56	0.25
Change in sales	0.15	0.11	0.22

Source: Company data

or full-time working, and gender, with customer satisfaction, employee satisfaction and employee commitment. There was a preference among customers for middle-aged staff, who also tended to be more committed. Part-time staff were more committed and customers were more satisfied with their service. Female workers were also happier in their jobs.

As Table 4.2 clearly shows, the strongest correlation (0.56) is between employee commitment and customer satisfaction with service, rather than the overall customer satisfaction measure. The correlation coefficients between all the items that were chosen to be in the final model are presented in Appendix Table 4.4.

4.4   Results

Figure 4.1 shows the final version of the case study attitude chain that was developed from the statistical model created as a result of our analysis. The figure shows the most important relationships between employee attitudes, customer attitudes and changes in store sales. The full model, which also shows the effects of region and staff demographics, is shown in Appendix 5. As stated earlier, any link that appeared weak was removed from the model; those that remain are all statistically significant. A positive relationship means that the items move in the same direction, both increasing or both decreasing together (represented by '+'), whereas a negative relationship occurs where one item increases as the other decreases (represented by '−'). The strengths of the relationships (equivalent to standardised regression coefficients) are shown on the pathways between the items.

Figure 4.1 The Attitude Chain

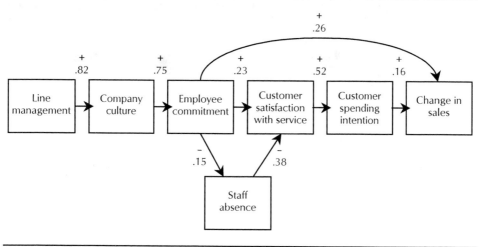

Source: IES

The weakest of these links appears to be the effect of commitment on absenteeism. However, the weakness of this link is misleading, and reflects regional differences that cannot be adequately modelled in the straightforward path modelling approach. For, as noted in Appendix 2, this approach assumes that the relationship between commitment and absenteeism was strong across most of the stores (−.38), but this relationship vanished for the 18 stores in the southern region, where it was slightly positive (.16). Commitment in the south was not as strong an influence on absence and the effect of this is to reduce the overall effect; however, in the majority of stores its effect was much greater.

Recall that interpreting any of the 'effects' depends on the assumed causal sequencing (from staff commitment to customer satisfaction to customer intention to purchase behaviour) being correct. The model shows that the perceptions of line management are strongly related to perceived company culture, which in turn is strongly linked to employee commitment. Employee commitment is a very important part of the chain as it is directly positively related to a change in sales, and also indirectly influences sales through its effect on customer satisfaction with service. The direct effect of employee commitment on sales levels is slightly greater than its effect on customer service satisfaction.

Employee commitment additionally acts through customer satisfaction with service to also change sales. This effect is then mediated through the customer's behavioural spending intention to result in an increase in sales. The effects of employee commitment also act on sales via staff absence: that is, as employee commitment rises absence falls. This effect is then transmitted to sales through customer satisfaction with service and spending intentions. A reduction in absence positively affects customer satisfaction with service.

Employee commitment, then, acts on sales through three routes in the model:

- directly on sales
- mediated through customer service satisfaction; and
- through reduction in staff absence.

5. Discussion

5.1 Data collection and management practices

This study was only possible as a result of exploiting the existing data sets made available to IES by the retail organisation acting as our case study. As our research uncovered during the scoping stage, employers currently collect and make good use of a variety of data, each fit for its own purpose but not necessarily transferable or appropriate for further analysis. We therefore advise those who are committed to exploring the links between their employees' attitudes, their customers' satisfaction and their business performance to:

- audit existing data collection processes and practices
- fully understand the purpose and utility of data currently captured
- ensure that information captured is 'fit for purpose'
- consider collecting information that is compatible both locally and centrally
- maximise the opportunity for including or revising survey items in order to capture data suitable for further analysis
- ensure information captured is also available electronically.

In addition, we feel it is vital to assign a fairly senior person to act as overall data or project manager who would probably need to lead a cross function team. This role demands a degree of technical expertise together with a sound understanding of operational issues, business and HR strategy and ideally should be undertaken by someone with considerable influence.

We believe this role is essential in ensuring data collected throughout an organisation is compatible, reliable and consistent. Although data captured must, of course, be fit for purpose and available to those at an establishment or local level, organisations could be disadvantaged if these data were not explored and analysed further. It is vital that all data managers understand the potential value of the information they collect and how their contribution fits with others.

5.2 Implications

Businesses need to retain employees and customers who are both loyal and profitable in order to remain competitive and encourage further investment. Only recently have employers begun to realise the potential of using attitude data together with other 'hard' business measures to gain a wider view of their organisations' performance. Intuitively, it makes sense that positive staff and customer attitudes are likely to result in favourable outcomes for the business. However, in the absence of any supporting evidence, such a notion could be viewed as no more than an act of faith, which does not translate easily into a sound business case for financial investment!

Our work shows that it is possible to relate employee attitudes to business performance consistent with other recent studies (Rucci, Kirn and Quinn, 1998; Patterson *et al.*, 1997; Caffman and Harter, 1998; Paradise-Tornow, 1991; and Schneider, 1991). As hypothesised, both staff and customer loyalty featured within our final model. Absence featured too, not as an outcome as initially predicted, but as an influence within the chain. However, we were unable to test the customer complaints and staff turnover data within the model.

Our final model illustrates that simply knowing customers and staff are 'satisfied' stops short of telling a far richer story. Using this model we gained further insight into what factors and behaviours may underpin and influence financial performance. We tracked the chain of events that actually influenced sales within our case study organisation:

- A change in sales was linked to predicted changes in customers' spending intentions.
- Predicted changes in customers' spending intentions were linked to customer satisfaction with service.

- Customer satisfaction with service was linked to employee commitment.
- Employee commitment was linked to company culture.
- Company culture was linked to employee satisfaction with line management.

In addition we found two other striking influences:

- Employee commitment had a slightly greater effect on sales than its effect on customer satisfaction with service alone.
- Not only did lower staff commitment result in higher absence, but high absence also reduced customer satisfaction with service.

Customer satisfaction is a broad concept and therefore difficult to define. Some customers might place a high value on accuracy and speed of response, whereas in others the quality of service is paramount. Therefore the various elements which underpin customer service are also instrumental in generating customer satisfaction and will vary considerably between customers and markets.

The final model showed that customer satisfaction with service *per se* did not necessarily result in increasing sales. The sophistication of the statistical analysis we conducted allowed us to establish the nature of the elements within customer service that mediated an increase in sales. Our initial model hypothesised that customer loyalty would mediate financial performance.

Customers' spending intentions was used as a proxy for customer loyalty and proved to be a strong mediating influence or link to increasing sales. Customers' spending intentions were therefore more reliable business performance indicator than customer satisfaction alone. This demonstrates the need for organisations to identify and understand further what drives the elements within the service relationship that customers value.

Our final model also clearly shows the influence that employee commitment can have upon customers' attitudes and behaviours, such as future spending, which in turn impact upon sales. Our initial model had hypothesised that employee commitment to service would feature as an influence within the chain. As the employee data made available to us had not captured information regarding staff commitment to service we were unable to test this prediction. However, our final model showed employee commitment to their organisation was a strong mediating link. Employee commitment offers a greater degree of insight than measures of job satisfaction alone and is grounded in employees having a sense of:

- ownership
- loyalty
- pride in their work

and can have a number of behavioural outcomes, such as absence or staff turnover.

There is considerable debate regarding whether employees who are more committed to their organisations have lower levels of absence (for example, Johns, 1997). Previous IES work has found absence to be lower among employees who were committed to their organisations. We had predicted absence and staff turnover to feature within our model as an outcome yet this study clearly demonstrates that employee commitment had a direct effect on employee absence and that this also negatively affected customer satisfaction with service.

If we return to our final model to understand the drivers of employee commitment further we see that it is mediated by what employees feel the company:

- values
- supports
- promotes

in short, company culture. Although we recognised the potential influence that company culture may have upon staff, we had not expected it to feature so strongly and, therefore, we had not included it as one of the links in our theoretical model. One of the real benefits of using statistical techniques such as pathway modelling to test relationships concerns the rigour that the technique brings to bear upon the data being tested, and our final model found company culture was a powerful influence within our attitude chain.

Organisational culture is partly a product of history and is considered to be the very essence of what a business represents. Organisational culture is often reflected and reinforced by the behaviours that organisations recognise and reward throughout the business. We found the strongest influence on company culture in our final model was employees' satisfaction with line management.

Until recently, people management had not featured significantly on the agenda of management development courses and many line managers came to their new roles from technical, functional or operational backgrounds only to find that they were also responsible for:

- selection and recruitment
- induction and training
- staff development
- communication
- performance management.

As predicted, employee satisfaction with line management featured strongly as a mediating influence within our final model. It shows without doubt just how instrumental line manager behaviour can be in relation to influencing sales, engaging employee commitment and influencing staff behaviour. Absence and staff turnover are usually the consequence of a range of complex factors, some of which are outside the control of the employer. However, previous research (Bevan and Hayday (1998), Cole and Kleiner (1992), Muir (1994), Reynolds (1990)) has shown how central the line can be in generating employee commitment and in encouraging staff to attend. This is particularly so when an appropriate framework is provided via effective absence policies, which might include:

- clear procedures
- communication
- return to work interviews
- recruitment and screening
- line management training.

The role the line plays in relation to managing turnover is well reported (Bevan, Robinson and Barber, 1997), as employees' perceptions and experiences of their organisation are largely shaped by their day-to-day contact with their line managers.

5.2.1 HR policy implications

Knowing that employee and customer attitudes can affect financial performance is a finding that is neither counter intuitive nor particularly surprising. However, our study has teased out a number of influences and behaviours which, in turn, were tracked to being influenced by line management. Most organisations recognise the pivotal role that line management plays within the business, and our model demonstrates just how influential they actually are in delivering business results through effective people management within organisations.

One of the most striking relationships our model uncovered concerned staff commitment having at least the same effect on sales as its effect on customer satisfaction with service. While we are not suggesting companies should not continue to invest in customer satisfaction initiatives, our message is to not under-estimate the value and business benefits of investing in employees too. Given that the line largely influences employees' experiences, we might ask how adequately organisations prepare, support and invest in the line in order that they might deliver the people management aspects of their role and what the implications might be for HR policy and practice.

HR is often challenged to demonstrate its worth in terms of business value. Our model provides a framework that supports a business case for HR to argue why employees should be viewed as business assets rather than costs. Increasing employee commitment has real business implications as an increase in employee commitment can independently increase sales. Using the IES model it is possible to show that an increase of one point in 'average employee commitment scores' (using a five point scale), represents a nine per cent increase in monthly sales per store. For this case study company a one point increase in employee commitment could lead to a monthly increase over £200,000. Realistically, to move attitudes by a whole point on average would be difficult to achieve, but even a small positive movement would have a worthwhile effect on sales. Conversely, a fall in levels of employee commitment will have a detrimental effect on sales.

In addition, a one point move in customers' intention to spend on the ten-point scale used to measure this attitude, is associated with a change of approximately four per cent in monthly sales per store (equivalent to a *further* increase of £90,000). A shift of this dimension would be unlikely even in the best of circumstances, but the figure does illustrate the value of even small shifts in customer behaviour. We urge employers to explore, understand and focus activities towards aspects of customer service that are within their control and also known to be capable of improving performance in their business.

Commitment from the top is vital in order to legitimise the view of 'people being business assets rather than costs' and the Sears example showed how this could be achieved, although it depended upon an organisation which was committed to bringing about change. Our work demonstrates the value of HR as a strategic, board level business partner directly involved with developing HR strategy that is driven by and aligned with business strategy. In such a role HR might benefit the business further by not just setting strategic objectives, but by also being instrumental in the development and deployment of well defined strategic measures. HR policies might then be translated into good management practices, which (with a positive culture, and high levels of employee commitment), in turn translate into improved business performance.

As products become easier to copy, competitive edge lies in a business being able to develop aspects of the business that are hard to copy or imitate and our model shows the role that people issues may play in financial terms. If organisations are really serious about investing in their people in order to achieve a sustainable business, then surely HR can and should be able to prove its worth and value. It has a key role in shaping employees' experiences via training and supporting the line in people management issues.

Our research arose from a growing belief that business performance may be strongly influenced by achieving high levels of customer satisfaction and retention, mediated through employee satisfaction. Our final model established certain aspects of employee commitment and customer satisfaction that influenced and mediated financial performance. From our findings we assert that HR should be considered as the vital 'cogs' within the business engine rather than become the 'missing link' in the attitude chain!

Appendix 1: Bibliography

Benkhoff B (1997), 'Ignoring commitment is costly: New approaches establish the missing link between commitment and performance', *Human Relations*, Vol. 50, pp. 701-726

Bevan S, Hayday S (1998), *Attendance Management: a review of good practice*, IES Report No. 353

Bevan S, Robinson D, Barber L (1997), *Keeping the Best: A practical guide to retaining key employees*, IES Report No. 337

Burke M J, Borucki C C, Hurley A E (1992), 'Reconceptualizing the psychological climate in a retail service environment: A multi stakeholder perspective', *Journal of Applied Psychology*, Vol. 77, pp. 717-729

Caffman C, Harter J (1998), *A Hard Look at Soft Numbers*, Gallup Organisation: London

Cole T C, Kleiner B H (1992), 'Absenteeism control', *Management Decision*, Vol. 30 (2), pp. 12-16

D'Archimoles C H (1997), 'Human resource policies and company performance: A quantitative approach using longitudinal data', *Journal of Organisational Studies*, Vol. 18 (5), pp. 63-72

Fisher C D (1980), 'On the dubious wisdom of expecting job satisfaction to correlate with performance', *Academy of Management Review*, Vol. 5, pp. 607-612

Fredendall L D, Robbins T L (1995), 'Modelling the role of total quality management in the customer focused organisation', *Journal of Management Issues*, Vol. 17, pp. 403-419

Johns G (1997), 'Contemporary research on absence from work: correlates, causes and consequences', in Cooper C and Robertson I (eds), *International Review of Industrial and Organisational Psychology*, Vol. 12, John Wiley & Sons: Chichester

Johnson J W (1996), 'Linking employee perceptions of service climate to customer satisfaction', *Personnel Psychology*, Vol. 49, pp. 831-851

Johnston R (1995), 'The determinants of service quality: satisfiers and dissatisfiers', *International Journal of Service Industry Management*, Vol. 6 (5), pp. 53-71

Heskett J L, Sasser W E, Schlesinger L A (1997), *The Service Profit Chain*, Free Press: New York

Muir J (1994), 'Dealing with sickness absence', *Work study*, Vol. 43 (5), pp. 13-14

Ostroff C (1992), 'The relationship between satisfaction, attitudes and performance: An organisational level analysis', *Journal of Applied Psychology*, Vol. 77, pp. 963-974

Paradise-Tornow C A (1991), 'Management effectiveness, service quality and organisational performance in banks', *Human Resource Planning*, Vol. 14, pp. 129-140

Patterson M, West M (1998), 'People power', *Centre Piece*, Autumn, pp. 2-5

Patterson M G, West M A, Lawthorn R, Nickell S (1997), *Impact of People Management Practices on Business Performance*, IPD: London

Reynolds A (1990), 'A training contribution to the control of employee absence', *Training and Development*, August, pp. 15-16

Reichheld F F (1996), *The Loyalty Effect*, Boston: Harvard Business School Press

Rucci A J, Kirn S, Quinn R T (1998), 'The employee-customer-profit chain at Sears', *Harvard Business Review*, Jan-Feb, pp. 83-97

Ryan A M, Schmit M J, Johnson R (1996), 'Attitudes and effectiveness: Examining the relations at an organisational level', *Personnel Psychology*, Vol. 49, pp. 853-882

Schlesinger L A, Zornitsky J (1991), 'Job satisfaction, service capability and customer satisfaction: An examination of linkages and management implications', *Human Resource Planning*, Vol. 14, pp. 141-150

Schmit M J, Allscheid S P (1995), 'Employee attitudes and customer satisfaction: Making theoretical and empirical connections', *Personnel Psychology*, Vol. 48, pp. 521-536

Schneider B (1991), 'Service quality and profits: Can you have your cake and eat it too?', *Human Resource Planning*, Vol. 14, pp. 151-157

Schneider B (1990), *Organisational Climate and Culture*, Jossey-Bass: San Francisco

Schneider B, Ashworth S D, Higgs A, Carr L (1996), 'Design, validity and use of strategically focused employee attitude surveys', *Personnel Psychology*, Vol. 49, pp. 695-705

Schneider B, Bowen D E (1993), 'The service organisation: Human resources management is crucial', *Organisational Dynamics*, Vol. 21, pp. 39-52

Schneider B, Parkington J J, Buxton V M (1980), 'Employee and customer perceptions of service in banks', *Administrative Science Quarterly*, Vol. 25, pp. 252-267

Silvestro R (1999), *Applying the service profit chain in a retail environment: Challenging the satisfaction mirror*, Warwick Business School: unpublished research paper

Stewart B (1999), 'Satisfaction guaranteed', *People Management*, 22 April, pp. 44-46

Tompkins N C (1992), 'Employee satisfaction leads to customer service', *HR Magazine*, Vol. 37, pp 93-95

Tornow W W, Wiley J W (1991), 'Service quality and management practices: A look at employee attitudes, customer satisfaction and bottom-line consequences', *Human Resource Planning*, Vol. 14, pp. 105-116

Ulrich D, Halbrook R, Meder, Struchlik M, Thorp S (1991), 'Employee and customer attachment: Synergies for competitive advantage', *Human Resource Planning*, Vol. 14, pp. 89-104

Weaver J J (1994), 'Want customer satisfaction? Satisfy your employees first', *HR Magazine*, Vol. 39, pp. 110-112

Wiley J W (1991), 'Customer satisfaction and employee opinions: a supportive work environment and its financial cost', *Human Resource Planning*, Vol. 14, pp. 117-128

Appendix 2: Preparatory Statistical Analysis

The primary statistical analysis used to assess the attitude chain hypothesis (the 'structural equations analysis' or 'causal model') was the end result of several preliminary stages of analysis. It is useful to describe these stages so as to clarify the extent to which the resulting conclusions depend on human judgement as well as strictly statistical criteria. Structural equation modelling rests on a number of assumptions, including: that the variables are normally distributed and are free from excessively 'outlying' values; that the relationships between the variables are linear, and show a joint normal distribution; that all relevant causal variables are included in the analysis; and that the direction of causal flow is correctly specified. The first two assumptions can be assessed from the existing data whereas the latter two assumptions can only be supported by theoretical means.

Stage 1: Variable selection

Although the hypothetical model of the attitude chain was originally specified on the basis of a theoretical literature review, there were still many decisions to be made about the specific measured variables that were analysed. As described in the main part of this report, new indices of customer and employee satisfaction were created based on factor analysis (although single-item summary measures of customer satisfaction turned out to be superior to the relevant summed scales). Only the best of these subscales, as assessed by internal consistency, theoretical coherence, and intercorrelations with similar scales ('convergent validity') were selected to be used in the causal modelling stage. There was also a wide choice of demographic variables available, from gender and age mixture to region and store size. As noted above, for a structural path model to yield unbiased estimates of coefficients, it is necessary to include all important, causal variables. Thus, our choice of demographic variables had to balance the need to control for all background variables that might be important, with the necessity to limit the number of variables in the final model (too many variables per unit observation lowers the power of the model, and in the limit can render the conclusions worthless). Note that both the choice of satisfaction scales and the choice of demographic variables were directed by judgmental rather than strictly statistical considerations.

Demographic variables were selected for inclusion primarily on the basis of their correlations with store sales, customer satisfaction, and employee satisfaction. This type of variable selection tends to overestimate the importance of the chosen variables, as the same sample is used for selection and final estimation. However, the specific relationships between demographic variables and the outcome variables of satisfaction and performance are not of central interest in this study. By including these variables we are confident that major confounding variables that might have masked the relationship between satisfaction and performance are controlled for.

Stage 2: Checking assumptions

Once the primary set of variables was established, each variable and pair of variables needed to be checked for a normal distribution, a lack of outliers, and for a linear relationship. Furthermore, it was necessary to check that the relationship between pairs of variables did not depend on the level of third variables. It is not uncommon for the relationship between variables X and Y (for example between employee satisfaction and sales performance) to depend on the level of Z (for example, the size of the store). When this happens, Z is said to 'moderate' the relationship between X and Y. Although moderated relationships or interactions can be estimated in both analysis of variance and multiple regression, they lead to special problems in structural equation modelling and should be identified early on.

Scatterplots between pairs of variables were examined to test for linearity, normality, and lack of outliers. Fortunately, no cases of non-linear relationships or strong departures from normality were observed, as these would have required variable transformations to repair. There were, however, a few outliers observed both on single and on pairs of variables, either because they had values that were substantially outside the normal range of the variables, or because they fell far from the line of best fit describing the relationship between two variables. When these outliers were examined in more detail, they were found to be stores which had opened or closed during the time period surveyed, and it was clear that they did not 'belong' to the distribution of stores that we were attempting to describe. Thus they were removed from the data set, eventually reducing the store numbers from close to 100 to 91. Finally, moderated relationships were examined by bivariate scatterplots with markers indicating the level of a third variable. For example, the relationship between employee satisfaction and store sales volume was examined by plotting volume against satisfaction, with markers for store size (small, medium, and large). In general, these plots revealed no moderated relationships. For example, the relationship between employee satisfaction and sales was slightly positive within *each* size of store (*ie* the relationship did not depend on store size). Large stores tended to have both the lowest satisfaction and the highest volume of sales, indicating that if store size was not controlled for, the observed relationship between satisfaction and sales would be negative, a misleading result.

Stage 3: Construction of causal models to test

The most difficult judgement to make about the causal model, and the most critical, was what variable to use to index 'overall performance'. It was clear that some measure of sales or profits was the 'gold standard' of performance. As profit values were not available, we used gross monthly sales. However, because raw sales figures represent (among other things) store size, store facilities, and features of the location (*eg*, inner city versus suburban) we sought an adjusted figure that represented performance *relative to* an internal standard of comparison, that of the store's *track record*. To obtain this adjusted figure, we used a least-squares regression to estimate current sales based on sales figures obtained one year prior. This predicted sales figure served as our internal comparison for each store, and the *deviation* from this prediction served as our adjusted performance figure. Thus, stores which were performing better than would be expected based on last year's figure received positive values and stores which were performing worse than expected based on last year's figure received negative values. Plotting these adjusted values against store size showed that we had indeed succeeded in removing the effects of store size (and, in the absence of any data on the matter, we hope that other confounding variables such as store location and facilities are also controlled by this method). Even with this adjusted outcome measure, our model still controls for all the demographic information available (*eg*, region, age group and sex ratio of employees) because these factors inflate some of the relationships estimated in the model (*eg*, some regions have both higher employee satisfaction and lower employee absenteeism because of regional cultures or local labour market conditions).

Even when the variables were selected and the performance measure chosen, there were still several smaller decisions to be made about the specific structure of the causal model to be tested. Although the hypothetical model drawn up on theoretical grounds specified a particular ordering of variables, there were subsidiary relationships that were unclear. For example, should regional effects only feed into the beginning of the chain (through employee satisfaction) or should they directly affect consumer satisfaction and even store performance? Such decisions were made on an *ad hoc* basis, guided both by theoretical considerations and by examining alternate models. This latter practice runs counter to the general assumption that structural equation models (causal models) are specified strictly on the basis of theory. However, it is very common in practical settings where the relevant theory may not be completely specified. In such cases, some amount of 'tinkering' is unavoidable and underlines the need for such models to be tested on new time periods or settings to ensure their validity. The only way to guarantee the robustness of a model developed through such incremental adjustment is to test it on a variety of data sets from a variety of domains.

Appendix 3: Scales Created from Employee Survey

Line management

5. I regularly get helpful feedback on my performance.
6. My manager takes my needs into account when making a decision that affects me.
7. My manager is helpful if I ever need support in times of personal difficulty.
8. I have a chance to grow and develop in my job.
9. My manager says 'thank you' to me for a job well done.
10. If I have a complaint about my manager, I am confident it will be taken seriously.
11. My manager values employees who make suggestions to improve the way things are done.
12. My manager is interested in the things that prevent me from doing my job well.
13. My manager will always make time to see me when I have a problem or need guidance.
14. My manager encourages me to improve the way I do things.
15. My manager takes the results of surveys like this one very seriously.

Reliability Coefficients

N of Cases = 42830   N of Items = 11

Alpha = .9139

Company culture

1. On the whole this is a very well run company.
2. There is a friendly atmosphere where I work.
3. Most managers have a lot of respect for the employees of this company.
4. Everyone is treated fairly whatever their race, sex, age or disability.
5. It's my ability that counts here, not whether my face fits.
6. The company cares about its employees.
7. The company believes that having satisfied employees leads to satisfied customers.

Reliability Coefficients

N of Cases = 55872.0   N of Items = 7

Alpha = .8492

Employee commitment

8. I would like to stay with the company.
9. I would tell people that this is a good place to work.
10. Working here makes me want to do the best work I can.

Reliability Coefficients

N of Cases = 59476   N of Items = 3

Alpha = .8103

Appendix 4: Tables

Appendix Table 4: 1 Correlation of employee features with variables in the attitude chain

	Female staff	Male staff	working full-time	working part-time	under 24 yrs	25-44 yrs	over 45 yrs
Customer satisfaction scale	.437**	–.437**	–.290**	.290**	–.437**	.575**	–.124
Customer satisfaction with service	.619**	–.619**	–.431**	.431**	–.517**	.592**	–.013
Employee overall satisfaction	.423**	–.423**	–.279**	.279**	–.226*	.277**	–.033
Employee commit-ment scale	.491**	–.491**	–.245*	.245*	–.393**	.496**	–.079
Absence	–.587**	.587**	.439**	–.439**	.492**	–.435**	–.183
Customer spending intention	.277**	–.277**	–.025	.025	–.354**	.473**	–.111
Change in sales	.007	–.007	.185	–.185	.042	.224*	–.411**

**   Correlation is significant at the 0.01 level (2-tailed)
*   Correlation is significant at the 0.05 level (2-tailed)
NB   There are no significant relationships with line management or company culture

Source: Company data

Appendix Table 4:2 Correlation of variables in the attitude chain

	Company culture	Employee commit-ment	Absence	Customer satisfaction with service	Customer spending intention	Change in sales
Line management	.82**	.69**	−.10	.20	−.01	.15
Company culture	1.00	.79**	−.18	.29**	.04	.20
Employee commitment		1.00	−0.43*	0.56**	.25*	.23*
Absence			1.00	−.65**	−.28**	.02
Customer satisfaction with service				1.00	.53**	.11
Customer spending intention					1.00	.22*

**   Correlation is significant at the 0.01 level (2-tailed)
*   Correlation is significant at the 0.05 level (2-tailed)

Source: Company data

Appendix 5: The Full Case Study Attitude Chain

The values on the pathways are standardised regression weights. From these it can be seen that the significant effects of region affect employees' perception of line management (0.21), and absence (−.45). There also appear to be different mixes of employees between the regions. The proportion of full-time staff is positively related to increased sales (0.25). Employees aged 25-44 years have a strong effect on customer satisfaction with service (0.28) and are the most committed age group (0.44).

Appendix Figure A.1 The full case study attitude chain

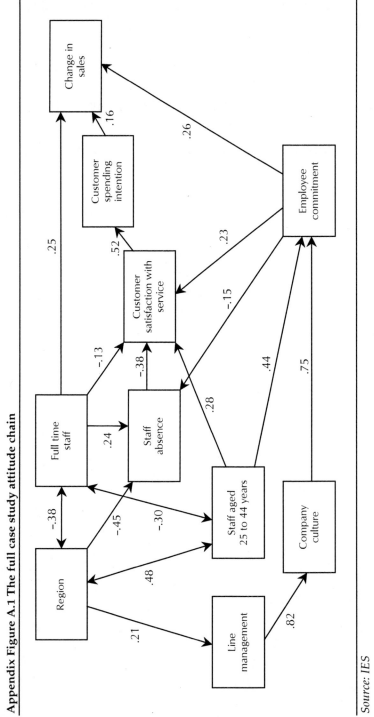

Source: IES

The Institute for Employment Studies